READING ABOUT

Diggers and Cranes

by Jim Pipe

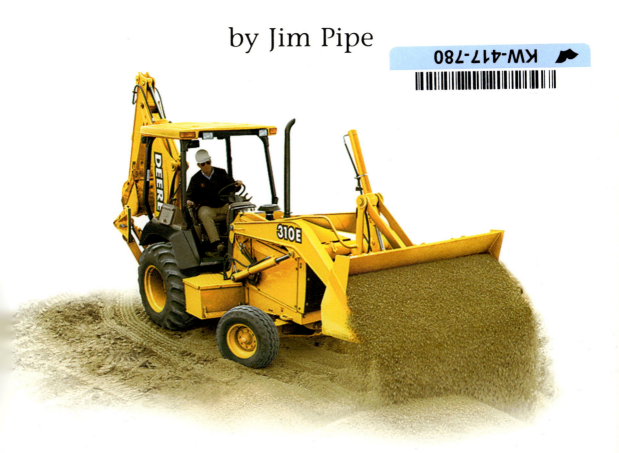

Aladdin/Watts
London • Sydney

Contents

© Aladdin Books Ltd 2000

Designed and produced by
Aladdin Books Ltd
28 Percy Street
London W1P 0LD

First published in
Great Britain in 2000 by
Franklin Watts
96 Leonard Street
London EC2A 4XD

ISBN 0 7496 3968 7

A catalogue record for this book is
available from the British Library.

Printed in UAE

All rights reserved

Editor
Leen De Ridder

Literacy Consultant
Jackie Holderness
Oxford Brookes University
Westminster Institute of Education

Design
Flick Book Design and Graphics

Picture Research
Brian Hunter Smart

Find out about diggers and cranes. They make hard work seem easy. Some of them work on a building site, like tower cranes and drills.

Bulldozers, scrapers and crawler cranes build roads. One special digger can do lots of jobs.

Diggers

Have you seen diggers or cranes in your town? They help us to build houses and roads.

Some diggers move earth out of the way. Others dig holes.

Digger

Crane

Cranes lift pipes, bricks
and other heavy objects.

These machines have the power
to get the big jobs done.
Let us see how they work.

5

What are the diggers doing on this building site? It looks a mess but the work has just begun. The diggers are clearing a space for new houses.

Building site

Could you knock a wall over?
This muncher knocks down
old buildings all day long. **Muncher**

The jaws of the muncher grab the walls and take a big bite. Crunch! The walls fall down.

Jaws

9

Big digger

Have you seen a digger make a big, wide hole in the ground?

It does this because the bottom of a building needs to be under the ground to make it strong.

The digger scoops up the earth and loads it into a truck.

Loading a truck

11

Drilling a hole

A drill makes a very deep hole in the ground. It works very fast.

The edges of the drill are sharp. It spins round and round to make the hole, like a drill your mum or dad use at home.

Electric drill

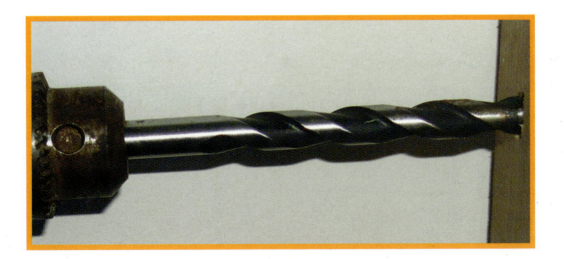

As a building grows taller, cranes carry bricks to the top. Would you like to work in this crane? You would sit very high up!

Tower crane

Small loader

See its arm grow!

This loader works in small spaces. To lift things, its arm grows longer and longer, like a telescope.

Mini diggers also work in small spaces. They dig a very neat hole so there is less mess!

Mini digger

These diggers are building a new road. The yellow digger moves earth, and the blue roller squashes the road flat.

Building a road

19

A bulldozer pushes earth out of the way to make a road flat.

Bulldozers are named after an animal. Can you guess which one?

Bulldozer

Scraper

This digger is called a scraper.

It scrapes away bumps in the ground and makes it smooth.

This crane is lifting a pipe into a ditch under the road. The pipe will take away the water when it rains.

Crawler
cranes

These cranes are called
crawlers because they
crawl so slowly!

This digger can do lots of jobs!

Do-it-all digger

It hammers.

It moves earth.

It digs holes.   It flattens the ground.

This digger has lots of power. It uses its bucket to shovel large rocks from the ground. But it makes a lot of noise when it works!

Mining shovel

Can You Find?

Some diggers have wheels, others have tracks. It is easy for a bulldozer with tracks to move across bumpy ground.

Tracks

Can you find the machines that have these wheels or tracks?

A

B

C

D

E

Answers on page 32.

Do You Know?

Not all diggers build roads or buildings. Do you know what these diggers are doing?

A

B

C

Can you match these diggers and cranes to their jobs?

1

Lifting

2

Pushing

3

Digging

Index

ANSWERS TO QUESTIONS

Page 29 – **A** comes from the bulldozer. • **B** comes from the small loader • **C** comes from the do-it-all digger. • **D** comes from the mini digger. • **E** is from the scraper.

Page 30 – Digger **A** is clearing trees in a forest. • Digger **B** is clearing snow from a road. • Digger **C** is working on a farm.

Page 31 – **1** is a digger, built for digging. • **2** is a crane, built for lifting. • **3** is a bulldozer, built for pushing earth.

Photocredits: Abbreviations: t-top, m-middle, b-bottom, r-right, l-left. Cover, 1, 2 all, 4, 10, 11, 20, 21, 24bl, 24br, 25bl, 25br, 28, 29tl, 29br, 30 all, 31tl, 31mr, 31bl, 31br – John Deere. 3, 6-7, 8, 9, 12 both, 13, 14-15, 18-19, 23, 31tr, 31ml – Select Pictures. 5 – Scania. 16-17, 29mt, 29bl – JCB. 22 – Corbis Images. 24, 29r – CAT. 26-27 – Digital Stock.